Daring to Date Differently

Relentlessly Pursuing Christ No Matter the Cost

HALEIGH WATKINS

WESTBOW PRESS®
A DIVISION OF THOMAS NELSON & ZONDERVAN

WestBow Press books may be ordered through booksellers or by contacting:

WestBow Press
A Division of Thomas Nelson & Zondervan
1663 Liberty Drive
Bloomington, IN 47403
www.westbowpress.com
844-714-3454

ISBN: 978-1-6642-0947-3 (sc)
ISBN: 978-1-6642-0946-6 (e)

Library of Congress Control Number: 2020920476

Print information available on the last page.

WestBow Press rev. date: 11/06/2020

Table of Contents

Introduction

We live in a society that constantly attempts to impress the idea upon us that dating someone is meant to be a casual affair, that it is more of a way to achieve instant gratification than to pursue a life-long commitment with someone who you truly love. The world claims that physical attraction is synonymous to love, that marriage is not something to look forward to, but rather an inconvenience or a piece of paper, and that by vowing to love one person faithfully, for better or for worse, in sickness and in health, 'til death do you part, you are choosing to be tied down and cannot enjoy any sense of freedom. Lastly, the world says we should do whatever feels right, whatever might possibly fill the void(s) that we have in our hearts.

I am here to tell you that all of those things that society tries to impress upon us are lies. Here is the truth: Dating is meant to be a way for you to evaluate whether or not you should marry the individual that you are dating. Love is so much more than physical attraction.[1] Marriage is a beautiful gift from God that acts as a symbol of the kind of relationship that He desires to have with you: bound by an intimate, unconditional, unending love.[2] Marriage allows you and your spouse to enjoy love the way God intended: freely, fiercely, and fully. Finally, there is only one

---

[1] 1 Corinthians 13:4–8 (New International Version; all subsequent citations are from this version unless otherwise noted).

[2] Ephesians 5:21–33; Jeremiah 31:3; Ephesians 3:17–19.

way to fill the void in your heart that doesn't seem to go away despite any of your futile efforts, and that is by having a personal relationship with God (See "The Best Decision That You Will Ever Make" for more information).

Before we go any further, I need to tell you a few things. First, you are important. You are enough. You are valuable. You are chosen.[3] You are forgiven.[4] You are "fearfully and wonderfully made."[5] You are wanted. You are special. [6] You are redeemed.[7] You have a purpose in life.[8] You are a child of the King, and you can do anything.[9] But most importantly, you are loved more than you can even imagine by someone who died so that they could have a personal relationship with you.[10] That person's name is Jesus.

The purpose of this book is to provide you with Biblical-based truths written in love about the realities of dating in a world that never ceases to try to lure you into settling for less than what God has for you. I have learned most of these things from the three and a half years my husband Christian and I dated. While I am married now, and you may be questioning whether my opinion is relatable or relevant because I am no longer in the dating scene, I finished writing this book while we were still dating and before I turned twenty. This book came from the bottom of my heart, from my passion to help other couples navigate the dating world by sharing things that I wish Christian and I knew ahead of time.

---

3 Ephesians 1:4.

4 1 John 1:9.

5 Psalm 139:14.

6 1 Peter 2:9.

7 Ephesians 1:7; 1 Corinthians 1:30; Titus 2:14; Galatians 3:13.

8 Jeremiah 29:11.

9 John 1:12-13; Philippians 4:13.

10 Romans 5:6–11.

In fact, many of the chapters were written as Christian and I faced challenges and sought the Lord to resolve them. Whether you have just begun dating or have dated for years, I believe that this book can be extremely beneficial in helping you and your significant other have a happy, successful relationship that is centered around God. Or perhaps you are single. If that is the case, then I believe that, by reading this book, you may be saved from potential heartbreaks. I want to challenge you and encourage you to dare to date differently than the rest of the world and to relentlessly pursue Christ no matter the cost.

I want you to know that I am praying for you as you embark on this journey. To the couples reading this, I pray that your relationship with each other strengthens and that, as you become closer to each other, you each become closer to Christ. I pray that, as you grow closer to Christ, you begin to see Him working in other areas of your life. I pray that you learn more about yourselves and each other than you ever have before.

To all of you, I pray that the Lord directs your steps and that you are open to whatever He tells you while reading this book. I pray that God uses this book to impact your life in a radical way and that you share what you learn with other teens that you come in contact with. Finally, I pray that the Holy Spirit puts a burning desire in your heart to take a stand for purity and to pursue Christ with all that you are. I am excited to see God move in your lives and I cannot wait to go on this journey with you. I'll be here every step of the way.

Love,
Haleigh

The Best Decision That You Will Ever Make

Our lives are influenced significantly by the decisions we make each and every day. Some decisions can be trivial, like what to eat, what to drink, choosing the amount of time you will spend hanging out with friends as opposed to doing homework, etc. Other decisions have a higher impact on our future, like choosing where to go to college, what career you should pursue, and where you want to live after you graduate. But besides those decisions, there is one decision that is even more important. In fact, I know that it will be the best decision that you will ever make: the decision to have a personal relationship with Jesus Christ.

I think it is safe to say that you can admit that you have messed up at least once in your life.[11] Maybe it was when you lied to your parents, or when you gossiped about someone. Maybe it was when you cheated on a test or when you said some very hurtful things because you were angry. The point is that we are all sinners, and that is where we run into a bit of a predicament. See, God is perfect and holy. In the same way that darkness cannot exist in the presence of light, sin cannot be in the presence of God. Thus, our sin separates us from Him.[12]

---

[11] Romans 3:10–18, 23.

[12] Isaiah 59:2.

On our own, there is nothing that we can do to get right with God. We cannot buy our way into heaven or do good works to make up for our sins.[13] But fear not, there is still hope.[14] Because He loves us so much, God sent His only son, Jesus, into the world so that "whoever would believe in Him would not perish but have everlasting life."[15] Born of a virgin, Jesus (God in the flesh) came into the world. The cool thing about Jesus was that even though He faced the same kind of temptations as we do, He never sinned.[16] He had a group of twelve disciples that went everywhere with Him. He performed a countless number of miracles, from healing the blind to raising the dead. Jesus taught people how they should live, and He did so in a way that was not condemning but convicting.[17]

During the time that Jesus began His ministry, a religious group of leaders known as the Pharisees watched Him closely. They were extremely perplexed by some of Jesus's actions, healing someone on the Sabbath (when people were not supposed to do any kind of work, according to Jewish customs), associating with people from lower classes, and claiming to be the Son of God. In the Old Testament, a prophet named Isaiah talked about God sending a savior, so they were aware that one was coming; however, when Isaiah spoke of Him, he talked about Him in terms of royalty, saying that He would be the Prince of Peace.[18] Naturally, people believed that God would use someone who was in a position of authority to overtake the government in order to bring salvation. When Jesus, a carpenter,

---

[13] Ephesians 2:8–9.

[14] Romans 6:23.

[15] John 3:16.

[16] Hebrews 4:15.

[17] The accounts about the life of Jesus can be found in Matthew, Mark, Luke, and John.

[18] Isaiah 9:6.

claimed that He was the Messiah that God had promised to send them, many people (especially the Pharisees) were not happy. In fact, they were outraged. They decided that they were going to form a plan to have Jesus executed in order to put an end to the revolution that had begun to occur as a result of Jesus's actions. One of Jesus's disciples betrayed Jesus, and He was arrested and put on trial. Jesus was whipped, taunted, had a crown of thorns placed on His head, and was beaten beyond recognition. Just like the prophet Isaiah said in Chapter 53, He never said a word the whole time. He was like "a sheep being led to the slaughter." He was then crucified with nail-pierced hands and feet. He looked down at the crowd in front of Him (the crowd that had shouted that He should be put to death) and asked God to forgive them because they did not realize what they were doing. Jesus died, a perfect sacrifice to the Lord.[19] He took on our sins and suffered in a way that we all deserve. Three days later, He rose from the grave just like He said that He would.

Jesus died for our sins. He took them upon Himself, and because of that, we can have salvation. It is simple really. Jesus is the way, the truth, and the life. No one can come to God except through Him.[20] He paid the price for our sins so that we could live with Him eternally.[21] All it takes is for you to repent, confess that Jesus is Lord, and believe that God raised Jesus from the dead.[22] You do not have to clean up your act before you ask Him to come into your life. He wants you to come as you are. He came to heal our hearts and make us new creations. What you've done in the past doesn't matter. What matters is how you decide to move forward.

---

[19] Hebrews 10.

[20] John 14:6.

[21] John 3:16

[22] Romans 10:9

Asking God to come into your life does not mean that everything will be easy or that you won't ever mess up again. There will be hard times in life, and we will make mistakes. Unfortunately, that is the way things are since we live in a sin-filled world. But I can promise you that God will be with you every step of the way, with arms wide open. By Jesus's blood, our sins are washed away.[23] God loves you unconditionally. When you ask Him to be a part of your life, He will radically transform you into the person He created you to be if you allow Him.[24]

If you haven't asked God to be a part of your life, I pray that you make that decision today. There aren't specific words you have to say because God knows your heart. Take this prayer and make it personal: "God, I know that I am a sinner, and I need you. Forgive me of my sins. I believe that Jesus died on the cross for my sins and that He rose three days later. I want you to be Lord over my life. I surrender all that I am to you: my past, my present, and my future. Please transform me from the inside out. I don't have everything figured out, but there is one thing that I am sure of. I want you to lead me for the rest of my days. Thank you for loving me and for offering a way for me to spend eternity with you. Amen."

If you just prayed a similar prayer, I can tell you that right now, angels are rejoicing in heaven.[25] You have just made the best decision that you will ever make, and I am so proud of you. I encourage you to let someone know about your decision—your pastor, a parent, or a friend you know is a Christian. If you don't go to church, then I encourage you to find one. The next step as a Christian would be to get baptized. Baptism is an outward expression of our inward commitment to Jesus,

---

[23] Hebrews 10:10–12; 1 John 1:7.

[24] 2 Corinthians 5:17; Ephesians 2:10.

[25] Luke 15:10.

which is witnessed by other believers. It is something that all believers should do in obedience to Christ since Jesus Himself was baptized, and we are to follow His example.[26] Start building your relationship with Christ by reading the Bible and praying. When you talk to God, pour your heart out and don't hold anything back. He already knows it all.[27]

If you have already accepted Jesus into your life but walked away at some point, I want you to know that it is never too late for you to return. In Luke 15:11–24, the Bible tells the story of a young man who wanted to get his inheritance from his father early. His father gave the young man and his older brother their shares of the inheritance. The younger son took his inheritance and decided to move away. Once he was there, he spent his money carelessly. Later, there was a famine in the country that he lived in, and by that time, he had spent all of his money and had to feed pigs to try to earn enough money to survive. The younger son was at his lowest point in life and decided that he had to act. He made the decision to go home to his father with the hope that, even though he had abandoned his family, they would at least let him work as one of their servants. As he neared the house, his father ran and embraced him wholeheartedly. The father even went and had his servants prepare a feast to celebrate. He also clothed his son in sandals, a ring, and the best available robe. The father could have treated the younger son harshly and reprimanded him for wasting his inheritance and leaving his family. Instead, he welcomed him with open arms and was glad that the son he had lost was now found. The way that the father treated his lost son is the same way God desires to treat us. Regardless of how far you might have run, the choices you have made, or the things that you have said, God loves you.

---

[26] 1 Peter 3:21, Matthew 28:18-19

[27] Psalm 139; Romans 8:27; 1 John 3:20.

He desires a personal, daily relationship with you. He wants to take your brokenness, your pain, and your sorrow and restore you. If you feel distant from God and want to return, simply repent and surrender your life back to Christ. He's waiting for you; all you need to do is take that step toward Him.

God has wonderful plans for you—plans to prosper you and not to harm you, plans to give you a hope and a future.[28] I pray that God uses you in mighty ways and that you share the hope you have found in Him with others. I pray that people see something different about you now and that, when they ask what happened, you can confidently tell them that Jesus came into (or back into) your life and that He offers them the same gift of salvation that you received. I pray that you seek Him first and that you do your best to live for Him. Now, go out and tell the world what He has done in your life.[29] I promise you that it will be worth it.

Reflection and Application

1. Take some time to thank God for how He has moved in your life recently. If you are currently in a difficult season of life, take some time to tell God about any fears, struggles, and challenges that you are facing.
2. Find a way to spend more intimate time with God—whether that is through a devotional book, Bible reading plan, journaling, or dedicated time towards worship and prayer.

[28] Jeremiah 29:11.

[29] Matthew 28:19–20.

How to Be Content with Being Single

One of the hardest things about being a young adult is trying to figure out who you are and then transitioning to a place where you are secure in your newfound identity. During our teenage and young adult years, we have a lot of transitioning and maturing that takes place. From making decisions about college and careers to choosing how you should prioritize your time, theses stressors can seem overwhelming at times. If you try to add dating into the mix prematurely, you will add even more stress, which will make things more complicated.

Let me start off by being perfectly clear: relationships are not a bad thing. In fact, we were created to be relational human beings. It is in our nature to desire relationships and being in them can be very beneficial to us. However, relationships (of any kind) were never meant to be used as a way to fill a void in our lives. Rather, they are meant to be additional blessings in our lives and reflect the kind of relationship that God desires to have with us. Sometimes, it can be easy to think, "If I had a boyfriend/girlfriend, then I would finally be happy, have a purpose, be important to someone, wouldn't feel lonely or unworthy anymore etc." It's as if we believe that a relationship will meet most, if not all of, our unsatisfied needs and desires.

I can promise you that there is only one relationship that will satisfy all of your needs, and that is a relationship with Jesus.

It's important that you are content with being single before you embark on the journey of dating for many reasons. First, if you are not content with being single, upon entering a relationship, you may find yourself becoming co-dependent on the person that you are dating. When you begin to feel the initial happiness and fulfillment that you were yearning for before you started dating, you might experience a sense of completeness. It's as if you've been searching for a missing piece, and now you have finally found it. You begin to spend more and more time with your significant other, looking to them to be your source of happiness, validator of your worth, and ridder of the loneliness you once felt. The problem is that they cannot bear the burdens of those roles that you need them to fulfill in your life. That job belongs to Christ and Christ alone.

Also, when you feel that initial sense of completeness after being in a relationship, the line between who you are as an individual and who you and your significant other are as a couple can become blurred, making it difficult to distinguish what your own identity in Christ is and being secure in that. This is not to say that this happens in every relationship. It is just something to be mindful of when dating. My point in saying all of that is that, just because you are feeling more complete, happy, valued, etc. when you are dating, doesn't mean that the only way to feel that way is by being in a relationship. You can still experience the fullness of joy in life as a single person.[30]

Another reason that your time as a single person is so important is that it allows you to make sure that you are a in right relationship with God before you attempt to form an intimate relationship with someone else. Paul talks about this in 1

---

[30] Psalm 16:11.

Corinthians 7:32–35 (New Living Translation) when speaking to a church in Corinth about marriage and relationships. In this passage, Paul says,

> *An unmarried man can spend his time doing the Lord's work and thinking about how to please Him. But a married man has to think about his earthly responsibilities and how to please his wife. His interests are divided. In the same way, a woman who is no longer married or has never been married can be devoted to the Lord and holy in body and in spirit. But a married woman has to think about her earthly responsibilities and how to please her husband. I am saying this for your benefit, not to place restrictions on you. I want you to do whatever will help you serve the Lord best, with as few distractions as possible.*

Paul isn't saying that marriage is a bad thing. In 1 Corinthians 7:7 (NLT) he actually refers to marriage as a gift from God; however, he wanted to make sure that the Corinthians realized that marriage is a huge commitment and should be taken very seriously. He wanted them to realize exactly what they would be getting into.[31] While being unmarried can be difficult at times, it gives you the opportunity to focus solely on serving the Lord while your attention is not divided between serving the Lord and meeting the needs of your spouse.

One of the difficulties that people face when they are single is that they view singleness as a prison sentence when they should be viewing it as a gift. I know that being single can

[31] At this time, Christians were also facing a lot of persecution, so adding marriage into the mix might have been too much for some people.

seem lonely at times, but I want to challenge you to try to use your season of singleness as an opportunity for God to continue to prepare you to be a spouse one day. I believe that once we accept our relationship status, we give God more room to work in our lives by submitting our dating lives to Him. If we are not in a right relationship with Him, how can we expect to have a good relationship with others? If your relationship with Christ is not where it needs to be when you enter a relationship with someone, both relationships may be good, but it will be difficult for them to be great. However, the closer you are to God, the more you will be able to love and serve others like Christ does with the Church, leading to healthier relationships with others.

Although it might feel like it at times, you do not need a relationship to validate your worth. In God's eyes, your relationship status does not define you. Your relationship history does not define you. Your relationships that you form in the future will not define you. What you do does not define you. Who you associate with does not define you. What you look like does not define you. Where you live does not define you. Who your family is does not define you. How old you are does not define you. What abilities you have do not define you. What does define you is what God says about you. He is "the same yesterday, today, and forever," and He will never stop loving you. [32] He is not restricted by anything that we view as a limitation. In fact, God doesn't even normally call the people that appear to be already equipped. Normally, he equips the called, the ones who society would deem "unworthy and unqualified". The real question is: Will you surrender and let Him equip you to be who He has called you to be?

---

[32] Hebrews 13:8; Romans 8:38-39.

Reflection and Application

1. a) How have your views about dating and being single been shaped by what society says?
   b) How have your friends and family shaped these views?
2. Have you ever found yourself trying to find worth in your relationship status?
3. What are some areas in your life that you need to surrender to God?
4. How can you use this season to grow closer to God and to love and serve those around you?
5. Find a quiet place that you can have some time alone. Once you are there, write out anything that you need to surrender to God, holding nothing back. When you are finished writing, spend some time praying to God about all that you wrote and listening to what he wants to say to you, and then shred your paper as a symbol of completely letting go of anything you were holding on to that you have now surrendered to God.

The Purpose of Dating

Before we begin this section, take a minute to think about the following question: Why do you want to date?

Dating is seen as a social norm which can cause people to feel pressured to date, especially if all of their friends are in relationships and they are the "odd one out." Some people say that dating is simply something to do for fun. I have personally heard people say that they want to date so that they can have someone to hang out with or so that they can post cute pictures on Instagram. Others worry that something is wrong with them if they aren't dating by whatever age they have deemed to be the "normal" time to start dating. People also view dating as nothing more than a casual fling, perhaps as a way to explore their options or just a way to hook-up with someone.

Despite those beliefs, I would like to suggest that there can be a different purpose behind dating—dating with the intention of marriage. This is not to suggest that you should be able to tell if you could see yourself marrying someone you are dating from the very beginning of the relationship. It is also not meant to put pressure on you to feel as though you shouldn't date someone unless you know that they're "the one." In fact, it is not uncommon for people to have met their spouse after going through a period of going on dates with several other people before entering a committed relationship. Instead, you should date with the intention of eventually wanting to become married and wanting to make a lifetime commitment to one person once you decide who that person is. Basically, marriage should be your end goal with dating being a step toward achieving that goal. You can take dating as an opportunity to evaluate whether you and your significant other should eventually get married. If you start to notice qualities about your significant other that go against the qualities you are looking for in a potential spouse, you may need to consider if you should continue pursuing a relationship with that person.

While some things can be worked on in the relationship—you and your significant other improve your communication skills, learn the importance of compromise, and determine what is and isn't okay in the relationship—other things such as continual problems with jealousy, neediness, and fighting constantly may be red flags that signal the need for you to re-evaluate the relationship. I am not saying that you should break up at the first sign of a disagreement or problems in your relationship. I'm saying that you have to be purposeful about being aware of how healthy your relationship is from an objective point of view. Having a trusted friend or family member help keep you accountable in your relationship may be a good way to do that since it can be harder to notice red flags when you are in the relationship.[33]

In addition, dating can be a way for you to see what works and what doesn't work in a relationship, which can potentially help strengthen your relationship with your spouse later on. For instance, when learning to ride a bike or play a sport, most people fail on the first try. It takes time, patience, and lots of effort and determination in order for you to become successful. The same goes for when you are in a relationship. You will come

[33] Go to loveisrespect.org for additional resources and quizzes if you would like help identifying and properly addressing unhealthy relationships.

across challenges (like falling off of a bike or losing a game). The important thing is that you take time to stop, recognize what went wrong, and adjust accordingly.

When Christian and I were dating, I found myself evaluating my relationship from time to time, realizing that there were areas that I could improve on. I struggled with voicing my opinion when I was upset, which led to bigger arguments that could have been resolved much easier had I spoken up when the issues first arose. In addition, Christian and I had to acknowledge that we had different love languages and, in turn, had to remind ourselves to be mindful of that instead of blindly assuming that we received love in the same way.[34] We also had to discuss what physical/sexual boundaries we thought needed to be in place and, even up until our wedding day, we made an effort to re-evaluate from time to time to see if we needed to change or increase our boundaries. Learning how to openly communicate with one another was crucial to the wellbeing of our relationship.

My point in saying all of this is that there is a learning curve that comes along with being in a relationship, and that's okay. I have been able to look back on all of my experiences and failures and have used them to help me grow in my relationship and in life in general. So, when you feel broken-hearted after a break-up, restless in a season of singleness, or upset after an argument with your significant other, remember that this is not the end. I strongly believe that God uses every single moment in our lives for a purpose. In Isaiah 55:1–13, God talks about how "[His] thoughts are not our thoughts, and [His] ways are not our ways." He continues to speak about how His word (the Bible)

---

[34] If you have never done so, I recommend that you (and your significant other) take the 5 Love Languages quiz. It can help you understand yourself and them better. Go to 5lovelanguages.com to access it for free.

never returns void by comparing it to how rain always waters the earth and makes it bud and flourish before it returns to the sky. What may seem like a dreary, rainy season in our life to us may very well be a time of refreshment and the beginning of a season of thriving in God's eyes. Sometimes, good things must fall apart in order for better things to fall into place. So, take courage; your story isn't over yet. Try viewing your time in the dating realm as a learning opportunity, a time that will help you be a better spouse one day and that will help strengthen your relationship with Christ.

Reflection and Application

1. What is your purpose behind dating or wanting to date?
2. What are some red flags that you think signal the sign of an unhealthy relationship?
3. a) Have you ever seen a friend experience, or have you yourself ever experienced the after-effects of an unhealthy relationship?
   b) How did you respond/react?
4. What are some challenges you have faced or are currently facing concerning dating and relationships?
5. What are some experiences that you have had that started out bad, but looking back, you can see how God used them for good?
6. Write a letter or note of encouragement to someone that is going through a difficult time. Dedicate time over the next week to pray for them and support them.

What Dating Should Look Like

> Don't let anyone look down on you because you are young, but set an example for the believers in speech, in conduct, in love, in faith, and in purity.
>
> —1 Timothy 4:12

When the Bible was written, dating was not a relevant cultural practice. Instead, people were betrothed or arranged to be married by their parents. It was not common for people to marry out of love (in fact, that was quite rare). Rather, people married each other based on if the marriage would be advantageous to both families that were involved. Since dating, especially dating the way today's society does, was virtually non-existent, the Bible does not explicitly provide suggestions or instructions on how Christians should date. This leaves many believers with lots of questions about how to date well in a way that glorifies and honors God.

However, even though dating itself is never mentioned, I believe that there are still guidelines in the Bible that we can follow to date in a way that pleases God. Before we discuss those guidelines, I do want to make it clear that the following guidelines are based on my own interpretation of Bible verses that I have made after careful consideration and prayer. I want to encourage you to study the verses and discover the meaning behind them for yourselves. What God may be telling me could be different than how He is calling you to live and date. My prayer is that this chapter is the beginning of your journey in discovering how God wants you to conduct yourself.

First off, Mark 12:30 says, *"You shall love the Lord your God with all your heart and with all your soul and with all your mind and with all your strength."* This means that, before we try to build a relationship with someone, we should make sure that we seek God above all else—above our family, our friendships, our academics, our extracurricular activities, our popularity, our success, and yes, even our dating lives. While having a close relationship with God does not mean that everything will be easy, God will give us the strength that we need to overcome any obstacles that we may face.[35] One way I've heard this described is: Put everything in God's hands and eventually, you will see God's hand in everything. I want to encourage you to fall in love with God and to fall in love with yourself before you think about trying to fall in love with someone that you are dating or want to date.

We just discussed the importance of putting (and keeping) God first in our lives before we start dating someone, but what about once we are dating? How can we act in a way that pleases God? In Galatians 5:22–23, Paul lists attributes, or fruit of the Holy Spirit, that we should desire and try to have as Christians. He described it by saying, "*…the fruit of the Spirit is love, joy, peace, forbearance*[36]*, kindness, goodness, faithfulness, gentleness, and self-control. Against such things, there is no law."* The fruit of the Spirit is something that we gain as we grow in our relationship with Jesus. The closer we get to Jesus, the more the Holy Spirit begins

---

[35] John 16:33.

[36] Forbearance means patience and endurance.

to work in us to make us more like Him. When you are dating or in any other type of relationship/friendship, it is important to evaluate whether you have those attributes.

Take a minute and ask yourself: Am I loving, even when I feel like someone doesn't "deserve" my love? Am I joyful regardless of my circumstances? Do I have a sense of peace even when I feel like everything is falling apart? Do I have patience and endurance during difficult times and when I face challenges? Am I kind to other people, even when they aren't kind to me? Is there a sense of goodness and gentleness about me? Am I faithful to my family, my friends, and my significant other? Do I have self-control? If you answered "no" to any of those questions or were unsure where you stood, I want to challenge you to pick one area and work on improving it this week. Also, pray specifically that God will help you grow in that area.

If Galatians 5:22–23 seemed a little too broad, you can read Colossians 3:12–17 (NLT), where Paul gives some more specific examples of how we can live in a way that pleases Jesus:

> *Since God chose you to be the holy people He loves, you must clothe yourselves with tenderhearted mercy, kindness, humility, gentleness, and patience. Make allowance for each other's faults and forgive anyone who offends you. Remember, the Lord forgave you, so you must forgive others. Above all, clothe yourselves with love, which binds us all together in perfect harmony. And let the peace that comes from Christ rule in your hearts. For as members of one body, you are called to live in peace. And always be thankful. Let the message about Christ, in all its richness, fill your lives. Teach and counsel each other with all the wisdom He gives. Sing psalms and hymns and*

> *spiritual songs to God with thankful hearts. And whatever you do or say, do it as a representative of the Lord Jesus, giving thanks through Him to God the Father.*

This passage is pretty straightforward, although that does not mean that it is easy to live out by any means. Forgiveness is crucial in dating and every other relationship that you are in. Forgiving people even when you don't feel like they deserve it can be difficult, but it is what we are called to do. Forgiveness isn't about what we will get in return. Forgiveness is about the condition of our own hearts. It can be very easy to fall into the trap of unforgiveness.

Sometimes, it feels like we shouldn't have to forgive someone unless they apologize or do something to make up for their wrong. When we have that mentality, we can end up developing feelings of anger, hurt, and bitterness towards people, which can overflow into other areas of our lives. When we hold onto unforgiveness, we suffer the consequences. My mom always told me when I was growing up that unforgiveness is as if you drink some poison but expect the other person to die. My prayer is that you make the decision to let go of past hurts and give them to Jesus. Forgiving someone does not mean that everything will go back to the way it was before, but it does mean that you are being obedient and forgiving people like Jesus forgave us.[37]

While the entire passage is important, I want to focus on the last verse that talks about acting as a representative of Jesus. In all that we do, in all that we say, we are supposed to live like Jesus. That is not something that we should only do when we

[37] Forgiveness does not automatically mean that trust is regained. Trust takes time, and after you forgive someone, you may still need to have boundaries put in place.

are at church or around other believers. We should strive to act like Jesus on a daily basis, regardless of our circumstances or who we are with. For me, that means taking time every once in a while to think about whether I act the same wherever I go and if I would act the way I do if Jesus was right beside me. I know that may seem a bit over the top, but my point is that Jesus wants us to be all in for Him, and it's important to make sure that we are representing Him well, especially in our dating lives. How we treat our significant other and how we act in our relationships, in general, are important. The question is: Is your dating relationship (or any other area of your life) drawing people closer to Christ or is it pushing them away?

Sometimes, specifically in your dating life, you may find yourselves in situations where you don't know what to do or how to respond. In the world that we live in today, we have worldly influences all around us through the media, the entertainment industry, and the people that we interact with on a daily basis. As Christians, it can be difficult to hear God's voice clearly in the midst of all of the other voices of the world. Trying to figure out how to date in a way that pleases God can be a struggle when everywhere around you, you see and hear people telling you something different. Paul, an apostle, having faced that struggle personally decided to offer some advice for how to respond to those situations in Romans 12:1–2 by saying,

> *Therefore, I urge you, brothers and sisters, in view of God's mercy, to offer your bodies as a living sacrifice, holy and pleasing to God—this is your true and proper worship. Do not conform to the pattern of this world but be transformed by the renewing of your mind. Then you will be able to test and approve what God's will is—His good, pleasing, and perfect will.*

When you are faced with the question of how you should date to glorify God or when you are overwhelmed by the secular messages that you hear all around you, remember this passage. Although it isn't easy, we should try to do our best to live like Christ, even if that means living differently than those around us. The ability to not conform to the world lies in the condition of your heart. I believe that if we seek to be more like Jesus and less like the world, the Holy Spirit will give us what we need to do so. Now, we may stumble at times, and that's okay. The important thing is to get back up and repent when you do and to continue seeking Him. When we are in a place where we desire to follow God, the Holy Spirit will reveal to you what that should look like, and my prayer is that He equips you to fulfill the calling that God has on your life to date differently.

Finally, as I have mentioned before, our relationships (specifically, marriage) should mirror the type of relationship that God desires to have with us. To be able to love others the way God loves us, we have to know what love looks like. 1 Corinthians 13:4–8 describes several qualities of Christ-like love. Chapter 13 dives into a more detailed discussion of the passage and how to apply it in our lives. For now, when you are finished with this chapter, take some time to read through the passage and think about what it means to you and how you can mimic it in your own lives.

<u>Reflection and Application</u>

1. Can you think of any other Bible passages that can be applied toward how to date differently?
2. a) Are there any aspects of your relationship/ friendships that you need to change in order to live in a way that pleases God?

  b) If so, write down two ways that you can improve in those areas and try to put them into action over the next week.

3. What do you think "dating differently" looks like?

Are You Ready to Date?

> Run as fast as you can towards God, and if someone keeps up, introduce yourself.
>
> —Anonymous

Deciding if you are ready to date is not always clear. There are several factors that are important to consider when making the decision to pursue a relationship with someone. The following questions discuss some of the topics that I feel are most important to think about before you start dating. Please take your time and do not rush through this section. Give yourself an opportunity to really reflect on the questions on your own. If you are already in a relationship, this section is a good way to evaluate where you are at in your relationship and if there's an area that needs to be addressed.

Are you in a right relationship with God?

I want to encourage you to take a moment to reflect on your relationship with God. Would you say that you have a personal, daily relationship with Him? Do you spend time talking and listening to Him through prayer and quiet time? Do you spend time reading the Bible so that you can know Him better? Are you able and comfortable with sharing about all areas of your life with Him? Those are just a few questions that will help you see how your relationship with God is.

The point of our relationships with people, specifically in marriage, is to imitate the relationship that Jesus wants to have with us. If your relationship with God is strong, you will be better equipped to have a strong relationships with others. I have seen how my relationships with other people improve when I am purposeful about my relationship with God. I have also seen how I have had problems in relationships when I am distant from God. When it comes down to it, I believe your relationship with God (or lack thereof) will ultimately influence all other areas of your life. It's your choice to determine what that influence will look like. Will you go ahead and date without making sure that you are in right relationship with God and hope for the best, or will you passionately pursue Christ in a way that helps your relationship not only survive but thrive?

Are you struggling with self-worth or a need for validation?

Sometimes, it can be easy to think that dating someone can help you find the validation or sense of self-worth that you have desired for a long time. Wanting to feel validated and worthy is not wrong. It's actually something that I think almost everyone has a desire for. However, I would not recommend looking toward dating as a way to fill those voids. Filling voids of validation or self-worth through dating is like trying to fill a bucket that has holes in it with water. No matter how much water you pour into the bucket, it will never be filled. Sure, a person that you date might temporarily make you feel better, but odds are, eventually, that person will let you down or won't be able to fill those voids for you. God is the only one that is capable of doing that.

When I struggled with self-confidence in the past, I found that there wasn't anything that anyone could say or do that would make me feel better about myself. I didn't start to feel confident and gain a greater sense of self-worth until I gave my feelings to God and allowed Him to work in my heart. Even then, it took time for me to reach a place of confidence. By reading the Bible and seeing who God says that I am, I was able to find my identity in Christ and gain a new air of confidence in myself. Below I have listed some verses that talk about how God looks at you. My prayer is that those verses will give you encouragement and that God will use them to open your eyes to how wonderful you really are, no matter how you feel about yourself right now.

God Says You Are…

- Forgiven ~ Psalm 103:12
- Known ~ Psalm 139:1
- Fearfully and wonderfully made ~Psalm 139:13–14
- Healed ~ Psalm 147:3
- Loved ~ Jeremiah 31:3
- Justified ~ Romans 3:24
- Set free ~ Romans 8:1-2
- More than a conqueror ~ Romans 8:37
- Accepted ~ Romans 15:17
- Renewed ~ 2 Corinthians 4:16
- A new creation ~ 2 Corinthians 5:17
- Chosen/Adopted ~ Ephesians 1:4-5
- Rescued ~ Colossians 1:13

Have you prayed about whether or not you should pursue a relationship with the person you are interested in?

It is always important to keep God at the center of your relationships, especially when it comes to dating. Just like you should pray before making any big decision, I think it is important to pray about whether you should pursue a dating relationship in the first place. By inviting God into your dating life before it even begins, you are taking a step in the right direction towards having a Christ-centered relationship. When you take time to go to God for wisdom and guidance before making a decision, go to Him with an obedient heart, willing to listen to whatever His answer may be, even if it isn't what you wanted to hear.[38] Having that mindset helps you put His will above your own and gives God more room to move in your life. When the time does come for you to date someone, continue to go to God with any questions, fears, doubts, or needs that you have. I promise that actively taking steps to not only include God in your relationship but to keep Him at the center will help you show your significant other and those around you the kind of love that Christ has for us.

Does the person that you are considering dating have core beliefs that go against your own?

It's completely normal to have differing views from someone that you are dating. In fact, that's a normal part of a relationship. However, there can be problems when someone that you are dating (or are wanting to date) has core values that go against what you believe. For instance, they may have different theological views (views about Christianity and what the Bible says) or different stances on "hot topics" than you do. Before

[38] Proverbs 3:5–6.

dating, but especially before considering marrying someone, it is good to have a conversation about each other's core beliefs/values so that you are on the same page. If/when you find that your potential or current significant other has differing views, you have to decide whether those differences are going to have a negative impact on your faith or your relationship. If your differences will not cause you to stumble or to doubt your faith, it's a possibility that the differences are simply matters of opinions. If they do or would have a negative impact on you, pray about if you would be able to continue to be in a relationship with that person even if their views never change.

Are there any red flags?

Another thing to consider is if there are any red flags. For example, is the person you are interested in or are dating controlling (checking your phone, asking for passwords to all of your social media, always wanting to know where you are, what you're doing, and who you're with, etc.), or do they show an unhealthy amount of jealousy? If that is the case, you do not need to be in a relationship with that person at this time. This is not to say that someone can't change. However, control/jealousy issues are signs of an unhealthy relationship that could potentially lead to an abusive relationship. If you are not sure whether there are red flags in your relationship, please look at www.loveisrespect.org for resources about the differences between healthy and unhealthy relationships.

What are your non-negotiables? Does the person you want to date meet those standards?

Everyone has their own set of "non-negotiables" for dating, or things that are "must-haves" in a relationship. For some, that can be little things like wanting to only date someone that is taller/shorter than them, the same age as them, enjoys the same hobbies, etc. I have even heard people say that they only wanted to date a person that fits the description of who they pictured they would date, saying they would only date someone with a certain hair or eye color. It can be easy to come up with a list of standards that you want your potential significant other to meet. Even though some standards that we set are done in a joking manner, it is good to really think about what non-negotiables you have when it comes to dating. Right now, I'm not talking about standards that relate to physical traits.[39] Instead, I want you to think of some standards that relate to personality traits and qualities of the person's heart.

Do they have a daily, personal relationship with Christ? Is their relationship with Christ evident in all areas of their life? Are they respectful to their parents and other authority figures? Do they treat everyone with kindness regardless of that person's social status? Do they act the same no matter where they are or who they're with? These are just a few questions to help you start thinking about non-negotiables on a deeper level. If the person that you want to date (or are currently dating) does not meet those standards, I encourage you to heavily consider if you should be in that relationship. If you aren't sure after reflecting on these questions, talk to a trusted mentor or parent that can pray with you and help you decide if the standards that are not being met merely go against your dating preferences or if they would have a significant impact on your relationship.

---

[39] There isn't anything wrong with having those type of standards; I have just learned that you have to be careful about not overlooking something/someone that God is trying to show you or bring into your life just because it/they don't fit into your expectations or standards.

Reflection and Application

1. What are other things that are important to consider before dating someone?
2. If you have any concerns about your current dating relationship, pray about it, talk to a trusted adult/mentor, and then address it with your significant other.
3. If you are not currently in a dating relationship, come up with a list of non-negotiables that you think are important in a relationship.

Being Equally Yoked

> Don't team up [yoke up] with those who are unbelievers. How can righteousness be a partner with wickedness? How can light live with darkness?
>
> —2 Corinthians 6:14 (NLT)

The concept of being unequally yoked has been a huge topic of conversation among churches for a very long time, especially concerning dating and marriage. Some people argue that dating someone that isn't a Christian is a good way for outreach, viewing it as a way to lead that person to Christ.[40] Others say that it isn't a big deal if the person you date/marry is a Christian because they don't think it has to be a non-negotiable or that it would have any effects on the relationship. There are also people that say they just want to be in a relationship with someone who says they're a Christian even if they don't reflect that in the way that they live. Finally, there are people that believe that Christians should only date other believers.

During this chapter, I would like to explore the topic based on what the Bible says. At the end of the day, being okay with

[40] This is commonly referred to as "missionary dating" which I will talk about more later in the chapter so stay tuned.

dating someone that isn't a Christian or that isn't at a similar place in their faith is a decision that you have to make for yourself. It is not my place to tell you what you can or can't do. I can only show you what the Bible says and explain what my interpretation of it is in the hopes that you will be able to make an informed decision.

Paul addresses the concept in 2 Corinthians 6:14 (NIV) by saying that it is not good for Christians to be "yoked" with unbelievers. But what does being yoked with someone really mean? A yoke is a wooden tool used in farming that goes around the necks of two animals and attaches to whatever they are going to pull. Since the animals are connected by the yoke, when one animal moves left, the other animal goes with it; when one animal sits down, the other must follow; etc. When the animals try to go in opposite directions, both animals end up struggling and are not able to go where they are supposed to. In the same way, if one animal is stronger than the other, it will have to bear more weight and responsibility, causing it to tire more easily.

Dating someone who is not a Christian or who is not at a similar place in their faith (doesn't hold the same level of importance of their faith as you do, isn't as spiritually mature, or doesn't live out their faith) can have the same results. Think of it this way: Let's say that you are standing on a chair, and the other person (who isn't a Christian or isn't at your level faith-wise) is on the ground. It will be much easier for them to pull you down from the chair so that you are on their level than it will be for you to try to bring them up on the chair with you. In other words, it would become much easier for you to become more like your significant other and potentially become weaker in your faith or start living in a way that would not glorify Christ than it would be for you to try to "save" them or help them turn from their old ways.[41]

That kind of effect does not necessarily happen automatically if you are not equally yoked in your relationship. More often, it is a slow fade full of justification and rationalization. For example, the person you are dating may curse, listen to music that is inappropriate, go clubbing, drink, do drugs, or do something else that you think is wrong or are not okay with. At the beginning of your relationship, you may be uncomfortable with that, but as time goes on, you find yourself thinking that maybe that behavior isn't so bad, maybe it isn't as big of a deal as you first made it out to be. Before you know it, you might also be engaging in the same behavior that you had once thought was wrong based off of your own previous convictions.

Additionally, if you are still on the fence about whether being unequally yoked is okay or not, there are a few things to consider. First, when having a relationship with someone that does not share your faith or is not at the same level as you, you will most likely experience a lack of intimacy that you would have when in a relationship that is equally yoked. Just like water and oil cannot mix together completely, it is extremely difficult, if not impossible, to fully connect with someone that is not on the same page as you from a faith perspective. As Christians, we are supposed to put God first in our lives above all else. That goes so far as to put God above your significant other, even when you are married. If you are with someone that is not a Christian or doesn't understand the importance of putting God first, a huge strain can be put on your relationship, and they may take it personally when you choose God over them. When dating another believer, however, the two of you can work together to

41 1 Corinthians 15:33.

surrender everything to God and keep Him as the top priority in your lives.

It is also important to think about the long-term complications that can arise from being unequally yoked, especially in marriage. If you marry someone that is not at a similar place as you are faith-wise, you need to consider how your differing views will affect other areas of your life. From deciding what God is calling you to do (which is difficult to do if your spouse does not believe in God or does not fully follow Him) to figuring out how to raise your children and come to an agreement on how or if you will teach your children about Christ, being unequally yoked can have a huge impact on the way you live. I say all of this not to judge you, but to make sure that you consider all of the possible consequences of being unequally yoked before making a final decision.

In the Old Testament, being unequally yoked and walking away from Christianity was a common occurrence. God recognized that, saw the way that it hindered the Israelites' relationships with Him, and warned them against marrying people that practiced different religions.[42] Time and time again, the people ignored God's warnings and instructions and suffered as a result of their disobedience. God did not instruct them to not marry unbelievers because he was trying to be mean or to make their lives difficult. He did so to protect their hearts and to help them stay in close relationship with Him by avoiding anything that could lead them to struggle in their faith.

Ultimately, our goals in life should be to be in a close relationship with the Lord, to serve Him, to build His kingdom, and to draw others to Him. In order to fulfill those goals, we have to avoid things in life that will cause us to stumble. When you are equally yoked, you can help encourage and challenge

[42] Deuteronomy 7:3-4.

each other to reach your goals and to live the way that Christ calls us to live. It is much easier to serve alongside each other as you work toward a common goal in the same way that it is easier for animals that are yoked together to go in the same direction. With that in mind, I encourage you to think about the importance of being equally yoked as you go about your week.

Reflection and Application

1. After reading this chapter, where do you stand on the importance of being equally yoked?
2. a) Have you ever been in a relationship or friendship where you were unequally yoked?
   b) If so, did you experience any negative effects or challenges?
3. What does being equally yoked look like to you?
4. This week read 1 Kings 11:1–13 to learn about how King Solomon, known for his wisdom, wealth, and success, was led astray after being unequally yoked.

Keeping Christ at the Center

She focused on God. He did the same. God gave them each other.

— Anonymous

Relentlessly pursuing Christ with a significant other can be one of the most fulfilling things that you can do in life, but what does that look like? How can you keep Christ at the center of your relationship, and more importantly, your life? How do you chase after God and rest in His presence in the midst of a busy life? These are all things that we are going to explore in this chapter.

First, in order for you to have a Christ-centered relationship with your significant other, Christ needs to be the center of your life. Initially, that concept can seem daunting, especially when thinking about all of your responsibilities. Some people think that putting God first in your life means allocating a place in your schedule to spend time with Him each day or a couple of times a week. While that is a good way to become disciplined in growing closer to the Lord, I believe that putting God first means surrendering all areas of your life to Him and inviting Him to be a part in all of it. Putting God first doesn't mean simply "making time for God" and checking it off of your to-do list. Putting Him first means letting Him see all of you—your struggles, fears, victories, anger, hurt, all of your highs, and all of your lows. Putting Him first means bringing Him into your busyness and your quiet time. It means being vulnerable and asking God to move in and through you and to shape you into who He has created you to be.

I like to think of having Christ be the center of your life like this: Suppose you write down all of the different parts of your life and put each part in its own circle like the image seen below.

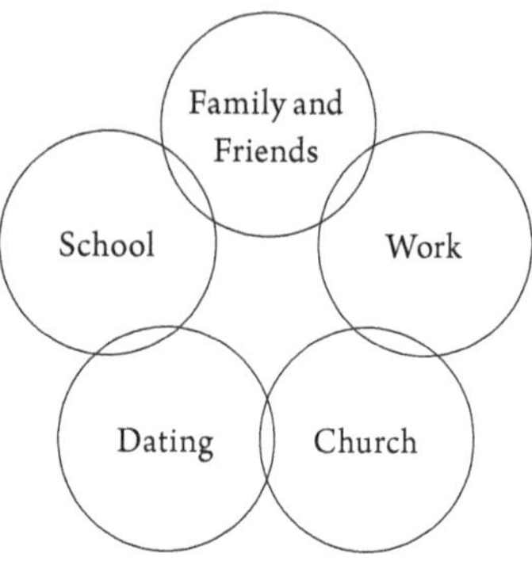

At a first glance, it doesn't look like you have much leeway to add in a circle for God in the midst of everything else. But what if you revised your circle to look like this:

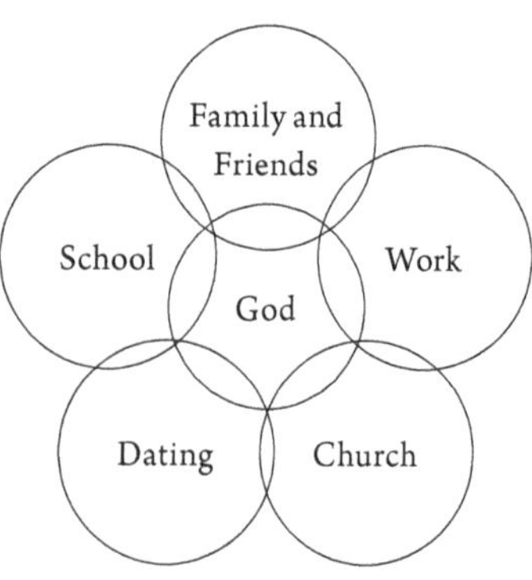

Instead of trying to add another circle on the outside, you can make God the center of your life and pursue Him in all of your circles.

This can look different for each person, but I do have some recommendations that might make it easier. Try to have a daily, personal, intimate relationship with God. Find time to pray (holding nothing back), to listen (quiet time to let God do some of the talking), worship, reading the Bible (finding a devotional book or a verse of the day and a devotion plan in a Bible app are great ways) and serving in your church and your community. Sometimes, that looks like waking up a little earlier, putting some worship music on in the background, and reading/studying the Bible, ending your time by talking and listening to God in prayer. Other times it looks like listening to "Lord, I Need You" by Matt Mahar on your drive to work when you're running late, praying briefly while you cook or clean, reading in your Bible app during your 15-minute break between classes, serving others by holding the door open for someone because finals are coming up and you can't volunteer at the church fundraiser because you need to study, and by the end of day you're so exhausted that you find yourself falling asleep in the middle of your prayer. We all experience different seasons in life, different levels of busyness, and different levels of stress. There is not a wrong way to pursue God or to invite Him into all areas of your life. I believe that God understands when we are stressed out and feel like we need 72 more hours in a day, so we talk to Him and seek Him in the brief moments that we can find in the midst of all of that. In fact, I think God is very pleased when you pursue Him, not in spite of your busyness, but in response to it. In the same way, God is very pleased when you are purposeful about spending time with Him in the "easier" seasons. No matter what season you are in, God wants you to pursue Him like a man that is dying of thirst in a desert pursues water.[43]

One thing to remember about having God at the center of your life is that you have to get rid of any idols that may be taking your attention away from Him. When people hear the word *idol,* the first thing that comes to most of their minds is an image of a golden calf or a statue of some sort that other religions use. While those are idols, I would like to propose that there can be 21st Century idols that we don't even recognize: the god of acceptance (idolizing popularity), the god of pride (finding your identity in accomplishments and chasing after success on your own merit), the god of busyness (being so caught up in your loyalty for God by serving and doing that you lose sight of your devotion to Him), and yes, the god of relationships (putting your significant other or the idea of dating higher than God).

I know that I did not list all of the idols that we can have in our lives, but my point is that they exist; they are anything or anyone we elevate to a greater importance in our hearts than God, and it is important to recognize their presence in our lives. Keeping Christ at the center of our lives means identifying those idols (whatever they may be) and getting rid of them. With that in mind, I think that the god of relationships is one of the most subtle yet damaging idols that we can have in our lives. Idolizing our significant other or our desire for a relationship over our relationship with God can happen quicker than we realize. It may start simply as getting caught up in the "honeymoon phase" of your relationship when you feel butterflies and you

---

[43] In saying all of this, I want to be clear that we should be purposeful about pursuing Christ and not put Him on the "backburner" of our hearts so to speak. How we do that may change depending on our circumstances, but our heart toward Him should stay the same.

constantly think about your significant other.[44] Before you know it, all you think about is your relationship, all of your plans are centered on your significant other, and all of your time and energy is invested in dating. When that happens, your relationship with God can be put to the side and neglected. That is why it is important to remember that a relationship with God will bring you more satisfaction than any relationship on Earth. By making it a priority to remove idols in your lives and by putting God first individually and together, you will walk in the call to dare to date differently.

Hebrews 10:24 says, *"And let us consider how we may spur one another on toward love and good deeds."* As Christians, we are called to challenge and encourage one another to follow God and live the way that we are supposed to by not conforming to the patterns of this world.[45] The same calling applies to dating and marriage. I encourage you to be purposeful about holding each other accountable in your walks and lovingly pushing each other past your comfort zones so that you can be who God has called you to be. In essence, help each other be the best versions of yourselves that you can be. Sometimes, that means having tough conversations, other times it simply means being each other's biggest cheerleaders and praying that God gives them discernment and strength as they follow the path that He is leading them on.

If you don't take anything away from this chapter except for one thing, let it be this: Keep Christ at the center of your relationship by putting His will above your own. Proverbs 3:5–6 says, *"Trust in the Lord with all your heart and lean not on your own understanding; in all your ways submit to Him, and He will make*

---

[44] These feelings are not bad. I just mean to point out that idolizing a relationship starts when you do not keep those feelings in check.

[45] Romans 12:2.

your paths straight." By being open and submitting to God's will for your life, you will be putting Him first. That isn't easy to do by any means, but it is worth it. Desiring God's will for your relationship means being willing to put aside your own plans and dreams and embracing what God has planned for you. The idea of embracing the unknown and walking by faith can be daunting, but God will be with you every step of the way. My prayer is that you take that leap and surrender your relationship (or future relationship) to Him.

Reflection and Application

1. How can you incorporate God into all areas of your life?
2. a) Do you have any idols in your life that are more important to you than your relationship with God?
   b) If so, what do you need to do to remove them and put God first?
3. Do you and your significant other pursue Christ individually and together?
4. Are you willing to put God's will above your own, no matter the cost?
5. Create your own circle diagram: one without God at the center and one with Him in the center. Put it somewhere that you will notice it often and use it as a reminder to put God first.
6. Take some time to pray about how you can keep Christ at the center of your relationship and how to follow God's will.

Communication is Key

> Communication to a relationship is like oxygen to life. Without it...it dies.
>
> —Tony Gaskins

Good, effective communication is key to a successful relationship. Not only is it important to be able to express how you feel to others, especially your significant other, but it is also vital to being a good listener and to making sure that you each are comprehending what the other person is saying. This chapter will focus on how to communicate well as a speaker and a listener.

One of the first things I would recommend is that you guard your heart by allowing your level of vulnerability and openness in the relationship to progress naturally and appropriately. For instance, it is not always the best idea to share your deepest, darkest secret on the first date. Trust takes time to build, and as you grow closer to each other, opportunities will arise to have those deep conversations. When you share intimate details about your life, your innermost hopes, dreams, and fears, you will naturally feel closer to someone. Proverbs 4:23 talks about the importance of this by saying, *"Above all else, guard your heart, for everything you do flows from it."* Your heart is special and is supposed to be protected. It is our responsibility as Christians not to give our hearts to someone prematurely and to be careful with who we allow to have a special, more intimate place in our lives. I don't mean that you can't be vulnerable with whoever you are dating. I just want to stress the importance of not trying to rush the process.

Guarding your heart can also be applied to a few other aspects of communicating with your significant other. One of those is being honest and straightforward with your (possibly potential) significant other. I think that it is important to be clear about your intentions behind dating from the very beginning. Are you wanting to date casually right now? Are you feeling ready for a serious, committed relationship? If you are in a relationship, what direction do you see it going in? These are just a few questions that I would encourage you to discuss. If you are not on the same page about your intentions behind dating, one or both of you could get hurt in the process, not realizing that you want different things.

In addition, guarding your heart also means being honest about how you are feeling and talking about problems that you are having in the relationship. Sometimes, it seems like a better option to be quiet when something upsets you because you think, "It isn't that big of a deal. I don't want either of us to get upset over something so small." This can be a smart thing when the issue isn't very important in the grand scheme of things because sometimes bringing up little things can lead to you having a critical spirit.[46] However, you have to be very careful with doing that because you can run into the problem of what I like to call the Snowball Effect. The Snowball Effect occurs when you start keeping all of the little things that are bothering you to yourself. At first, the problems are small (like a ball of

[46] Proverbs 10:19; My sister always says, "If what is bothering/worrying you won't matter in five years, don't waste five minutes dealing with it."

snow as it initially rolls down a hill towards you), but before you know it, your anger/frustration/sadness gain intensity and you explode (the snowball grows as you move faster and faster down the hill before it finally hits you).

Internalizing your feeling may seem like a good approach at the time, especially if you like to avoid confrontation, but it can actually hurt you and your significant other even more down the line. Christian and I realized this early on in our relationship. When either of us were upset, we would keep it to ourselves until we couldn't hold it in any longer. By the time we expressed how we really felt, our feelings were much stronger since they had been pent up. More than likely, the problems could have been handled much easier had we been honest from the start. Now, we do our best to bring things up in the moment, if possible. Depending on the circumstances or the situation, we may decide to take some time to think and pray about it before we have a discussion, but we do our best to initially address it when it happens.

One thing to consider if you are struggling to tell your significant other how you feel is this: How can they help you, support you, or fix the problem if they don't know what it is? Being able to communicate openly is a key factor in any type of relationship. I know that confrontation and conflict can be intimidating, but having disagreements is a normal part of a relationship. Having a fight doesn't mean that you automatically need to break up with your significant other. It just means that you are communicating. It's virtually impossible for you to agree on every single thing since you're two completely different people. In fact, for couples in long-term relationships who say that they've never had a disagreement, I'd say that they may want to see if they are truly communicating about everything.

As far as having disagreements go, it is vital that you understand how to argue well. The best advice I can give on how to do that is to attack the problem, not each other. The way I see it, when you get married, you make the commitment to be with each other for the rest of your lives. That means that you can't end the marriage when things get difficult; you need to work together to find a solution. Your spouse will be your teammate, not your opponent, even though it may feel like it at times.

A good way to argue well is by using "I" statements when describing something that's bothering you. For example, it would be better to say, "I feel that my concerns aren't being heard," instead of, "You never listen to me, and you're not really listening to me now." Another example would be saying, "I feel unimportant when we make plans, but you end up canceling to hang out with your friends." Instead of "You don't make me a priority, and you clearly don't care about me." Using "I" statements helps avoid placing blame and making people feel defensive. "I" statements can also help you better explain things from your point of view in a respectful way that makes your feelings clear.

It's important to remember that both of your perspectives and feelings should be validated and vocalized, whether you agree with each other or not. Even if your significant other's perspective doesn't seem accurate, the reality of the situation is that that's how they feel, so the focus should be on how to resolve their perceived problem. When having a disagreement and vocalizing how you feel, take into consideration how and what you are saying. James, a follower of Jesus, instructed Christians to "*be quick to listen, slow to speak, and slow to become angry.*"[47] I try to use the THINK acronym before I speak, asking myself the following questions: Is it True? Is it Helpful? Is it Inspiring? Is it Necessary? Is it Kind? Our words are very powerful. In fact, Proverbs 18:21(NLT) says that the tongue is so powerful that

---

[47] James 1:19.

it can bring death or life. We should strive to speak life in all of our conversations and in all of our disagreements/arguments.

Good communication is something that develops over time in any relationship. It does not happen overnight, and there will always be times that disagreements come up. The good news is that through being purposeful about being honest and open about your feelings and intentions, THINKing before you speak, and fighting problems instead of the person you're arguing with, you can develop stronger, more positive communication skills. It isn't always easy but communicating well can significantly improve your relationship and/or friendships.

Reflection and Application

1. a) Have you ever been hurt by not guarding your heart in the past?
   b) If so, what would you have done differently?
2. a) What are your intentions behind wanting to date someone?
   b) Have you made those intentions clear if you are interested in or dating someone?
3. Are you more of an internalizing or expressive person when you are bothered by something?
4. Is there any way that you can communicate better or more positively than you are currently?
5. Practice using "I" statements and see if that leads to better communication the next time you have an argument with someone.

Worth the Wait

I know you might be thinking that you are about to read the same speech about sex and purity that you've probably heard a countless number of times. My hope is that I prove you wrong. I am not here to make you feel judged or condemned. I am not here to tell you about all of the statistics concerning waiting to have sex until you are married versus not waiting.[48] I am here to tell you what God thinks about sex, love, marriage, and purity, and how following His word or disobeying it can affect you.

Before I go any further, I want to say to those of you that may be experiencing guilt and shame from "going too far" or from having sex, God offers healing, forgiveness, and freedom no matter what. He loves you unconditionally and is waiting for you with arms wide open. You can never make too many mistakes or do something bad enough to separate you from His love.[49] You can make the choice for purity now regardless of what your past looks like because God is bigger than your past. He desires to restore you, to have a relationship with you, and to show you how to live like Jesus.

For those of you that are on the other end of the spectrum and are afraid, apprehensive, or feel like you have a negative view

---

[48] Not only is waiting very important from a Biblical perspective, there are reasons from a clinical perspective that support saving sex for marriage as well such as prevention of STIs.

[49] Romans 8:38–39.

on sex, I am here to tell you that sex is an amazing gift from God that He has used to show people (within the safety and sanctity of marriage) the type of intimate relationship that He desires to have with you. I want to be very clear that sex is not bad. It is simply supposed to be enjoyed between a husband and wife. Sometimes, people can experience fear or develop a negative view about sex because they hear so much about how having sex outside of marriage is wrong that they do everything they can to avoid it entirely out of fear of messing up.

When that happens, it can be difficult to shift from a "sex is bad, dirty, etc." mentality before marriage to fully embracing sexual intimacy and freedom with your spouse once you are married. That is why I believe that it is important to realize that there is nothing wrong with sex, but we also need to recognize that God designed it to only be okay for married couples. So for those of you that feel like this section is relatable, I want you to know that I am praying that your eyes are opened to the truth about sex the way God intended it to be, leading you to a place of freedom and a positive view about sex and purity.

I'm sure you can list off several reasons of why we are told to wait to have sex until marriage. Warnings about sexually transmitted infections (STIs), pregnancy, baggage that can result from having multiple partners, and the seriousness of the emotional connections that are formed during sex[50] are addressed pretty heavily. But what if I told you that, while those warnings are important, there is a reason to wait even if all of the warnings proved to be false and there were no negative worldly repercussions for having sex outside of marriage? The real reason to save sex (and other forms of sexual/physical intimacy)

[50] When you have sex, your body releases oxytocin which is a chemical used for bonding that is also released when a woman gives birth. Some people argue that sex is purely physical, but I believe it becomes that way when they are desensitized to the emotional connection that God designed for sex.

for marriage even if you don't think that any of the other reasons are valid is because the Bible is very clear that God designed sex for marriage and marriage alone.

In the very beginning, God created Adam and later, Eve. Genesis 2:24 explains how God decided that in marriage, a man and woman are supposed to leave their families, become united, and transition from a mindset of "me to we" (becoming one flesh). Throughout the Bible, it is clear that that includes intimacy on all levels: spiritual, emotional, and yes, physical. The book of Song of Solomon demonstrates the type of physical intimacy that God intended to exist in marriage: an unashamed, unreserved, and passionate intimacy that is built on a solid foundation of trust, respect, selflessness, safety, and unconditional love. The husband and wife in the passage enjoyed sex freely and fully without any guilt because it was the way that God intended for it to be.

I like to think of God's purpose behind saving sex for marriage like this: Suppose when you were younger, your parents planned on giving you a car for your sixteenth birthday, and it's being kept in your garage until you are old enough to drive it. They are very clear that when you turn sixteen, the car is yours to enjoy as long as you drive safely and according to the law. One day you decide that even though you are only thirteen, you want to drive the car. After all, you've heard how fun driving is, you think that your parents don't understand, and the rules they created aren't accurate so why not drive the car now? The problem is that because you decided to drive the car before you should have, you got in an accident and your parents have grounded you for three months. Driving a car is not bad, but the timing of when you drive and the guidelines surrounding driving are important and are intended with your benefit and protection in mind. Although it doesn't always make sense at the time, we have to trust that God's judgment is better than our own and that He has our best interests in mind.

If you are wondering where in the Bible God actually addresses his intentions and design regarding sex, take a look at 1 Thessalonians 4:3. It says, *"it is God's will that you should be sanctified: that you should avoid sexual immorality."* Sexual immorality refers to any form of sexual activity outside of marriage including lust, adultery, pornography, touching someone or allowing someone else to touch you anywhere that undergarments cover (yes, even if you keep your clothes on), etc. Paul gives more in-depth support for why we should avoid sexual immorality 1 Corinthians 6:18–20 saying,

> *Flee from sexual immorality. All other sins a person commits are outside the body, but whoever sins sexually, sins against their own body. Do you not know that your bodies are temples of the Holy Spirit, who is in you, whom you have received from God? You are not your own; you were bought at a price. Therefore, honor God with your bodies.*

The first thing to recognize in that passage is the word *flee.* When talking about other sins, the Bible often uses phrases such as "turn away from" or "put off old ways." Advising people to flee from sexual immorality indicates the seriousness of the issue and emphasizes how difficult it can be to stop or turn away from old habits. Fighting for purity and working towards glorifying God by avoiding sexual immorality is not something that should be taken lightly. It is not an easy battle, so we must be vigilant. In saying that, God can help us stand strong and resist temptation, even when it is extremely hard not to give in to your desires.

The second thing to recognize is that sexual immorality is a sin "against your own body." While some sins only have fleeting consequences/effects, sexual sin can have a lasting impact on you and your future relationships. Also, our bodies are "temples of the Holy Spirit," so we should be respectful and do our best to be good stewards of what God has given us. Before you head down a path that you shouldn't go, think about the consequences and about whether your actions will honor or dishonor God.

Those were just a few points that can be used to show support for God's design for sex. I know right now you may be feeling like all you read were a bunch of rules and regulations, but I promise you that saving sex for marriage, fighting for purity in your hearts, minds, and actions, and treating your bodies like they are temples of God will be worth it in the end. When you are married, all of the difficulties and frustrations you faced, all of the waiting will be worth it knowing that you walked in obedience to Christ. I know this because, after waiting and fighting for purity in our dating relationship, Christian and I did end up waiting to have sex until we were married by the grace of God, and it was worth it for us.

But even if there were no extra benefits for waiting and even if we don't understand the reasons behind the "why," we are called to obey God's instructions and trust that He has our best interests in mind. We shouldn't obey God because of what we can get out of it. We should obey Him because that is what we are called to do as followers of Jesus. I realize that accepting that can be frustrating when the world says that waiting doesn't matter and when giving in to having sex is so easy, but God never said that following his word would be easy. Paul, one of the most influential people in the Bible, struggled with sin as a strong

Christian.[51] No one, not even the people that seem like they have it all together and are grounded in their faith, is exempt from or above experiencing temptation, especially sexually. Believing that you could never be affected by sexual temptation is a dangerous mindset to have. We cannot face temptation on our own merit or abilities but by the grace and power that we have in Jesus. Realizing that we can't fight this battle alone is one of the first steps in submitting our struggles to God and fighting for our purity.

I say all of this not to be discouraging but to spark a real conversation about the hard truth of what striving to glorify God in all areas of our relationships looks like. The truth is that being a follower of Jesus and not conforming to the world,[52] whether that be in your dating relationship or another area of your life, will cost you. Being a Christian and having a heart completely sold out to Christ will cost you. Knowing that, you have to make the decision to either dare to date differently the way that God intended or to live the way the world tells you to; that choice is completely up to you. That being said, my prayer is that as you begin to build a stronger relationship with God, your desires begin to shift to His desires and that the Holy Spirit equips you to dare to date differently, no matter how difficult that may be. Because at the end of the day, we are not called to understand, we are called to be obedient and to live for Christ.

Reflection and Application

1. a) When is a time in your life that God instructed you to be patient and wait?
   b) Were you able to see afterward how waiting was worth it?

---

[51] Romans 7:14–25.

[52] Romans 12:2.

2. How does the world paint a different picture about sex than the Bible?
3. If you are still uncertain about saving sex for marriage or if you are struggling with feeling shame from your sexual past or are having a negative view about sex, please reach out to a trusted friend or mentor and ask them to pray with you and help you do some more research about how God views sex.
4. Would daring to date differently change the way you currently view sex?

Boundaries in Dating

Disclaimer: this will be a longer chapter, but that is because this is something that I feel needs to be talked about more in-depth. It can be brushed under the rug in the Christian culture because it makes people feel uncomfortable, but that isn't why I'm writing this. This chapter is meant to help you navigate boundaries in dating, so please give it a chance.

If you've read Chapter 9: Worth the Wait, you know that the Bible is clear that God designed sex to be within the confines of marriage. However, the Bible does not specifically address what physical boundaries in dating relationships should be (aside from a few things the Bible clearly states are for marriage), leaving many Christians confused about what the "right" way to date looks like. Trying to figure out boundaries in dating is especially difficult when society tells us that we should do whatever feels good regardless of what the Bible says.

I can honestly say that, while I was dating Christian, I had been studying and praying about boundaries in dating for a very long time, and it was still confusing at times. We didn't always stay in line with our boundaries, and there were times that we had to repent and seek the Lord's guidance as we fought for our purity. I thought that the easiest thing would be to have a concrete answer of what's okay. If I could stay far away from the line of what was wrong, I didn't have to worry about messing up or displeasing God. However, I've grown to realize that it is crucial to examine your heart and boundaries from time to time because it is so easy to fall into sin and not recognize it until you go farther than you should have. I've also learned that, while there are some clear boundaries that are distinctly for marriage based on biblical principles, which we will discuss later, other boundaries are shaped by each person's personal convictions.

Many people ask the question, "How far is too far?" when trying to figure out what their boundaries should be. The problem is that asking that can imply an underlying desire of you wanting to do as much as you can get away with, which you have to be careful to avoid. As Christians, our hearts should be focused on what will please God, not what is most beneficial and/or satisfying for us. This is a tough concept to grasp, but at the end of the day, our lives are not about us and our desires. Our lives are about living for Jesus and dying to ourselves no matter how difficult or costly that might be. When we have hearts fully surrendered to God, the Holy Spirit moves in our lives and transforms our hearts to be in line with His. In doing so, our desires stem from God's desires which helps us to follow His will, even when our flesh struggles.

Before we go any further, I want to be very clear that I say all of this without any judgment. This is a very sensitive topic that is not easy to figure out. If you have had sex or have "gone too far," know that God is still there for you and loves you unconditionally. We all fall short of His glory;[53] the important thing is getting back up and turning to Christ when we do mess up. It is never too late to make the decision to dare to date differently and pursue purity. And purity is so much more than what you've done sexually in the physical sense. Purity is about the condition of your body, mind, and soul; it is a battle

---

[53] Romans 3:23.

that continues throughout our entire lives, even when you're married.

When I say that you have to be careful about asking, "How far is too far?" I say it to serve as a reminder to check your heart. Doing that helps keep you accountable to make sure you are following what God wants for you, not what your flesh wants. I know from experience that fighting for purity and maintaining physical boundaries that please God can be extremely difficult. Messages promoting the hookup culture, "living your best life," and instant gratification fueled by the mantra that "you only live once" are everywhere you turn. Movies, TV shows, music, college, and peers are constantly adding to the pressure that we have as Christian young adults to give in to temptation and conform to society. After a while, the decision to wait to have sex until marriage can seem pointless or not worth the frustration, both feelings stemming from lies that Satan tries to tell us. I believe that if you don't lean on God, keep Him at the center of your life and your relationship, and learn how to recognize, call out, and refute the lies of the enemy, it will be virtually impossible to not give in to sexual temptation and sin.

In the midst of the internal struggle between doing the right thing and doing the easy thing, we can slowly fall into the trap of justification and rationalization. It may not be blatant, but rather small doubts from time to time like, "Maybe going a little farther one time won't hurt as long as it's only once," "Maybe we did cross some boundaries that we shouldn't have, but we aren't actually having sex so at least we're doing better than some people," "I think I may be feeling conviction, but it could just be feeling nervous about crossing a boundary for the first time," and "My significant other, who is also a Christian and wants to fight for their purity, says they don't think what we are doing is inappropriate, so I'm probably just overthinking things."

To address the first thought, I believe that thinking that you can go somewhere physically only once and then never have the desire to do that again until you are married is misguided. First, if you are having that thought, the idea that you think it should be something that can only be allowed once in order for it to be acceptable raises a red flag that it's probably not something you should be doing at all. Second, once you cross physical boundaries, it is natural for things to progress even further. By crossing a boundary that you shouldn't (yes, even if it's only one time), you are opening the door for further temptation.

To address that second thought of allowing certain sexual behaviors since you still aren't having sex, there are things besides intercourse that are not okay in a dating relationship, period. Many people believe the lie that as long as there isn't penetration, there's no harm, no foul. But God calls us to do more than aim for technical virginity. I had questions about what the clear boundaries should be myself, and books I read were very vague, so I'll be blunt about what I wish someone had said to me.[54] I believe that maintaining purity of our hearts and bodies also means not participating in, entertaining, or giving into lustful thoughts, adultery, pornography, masturbation, touching someone or allowing someone else to touch you inappropriately[55] with or without clothes on, oral sex, sending nudes, sleeping in bed together, grinding/humping with clothes

[54] I realize that some of this is very blunt; however, I believe that dancing around the subject of sex is what causes people to struggle more in the first place, which is why it is important to have open, straightforward discussions.

[55] To be clear, places that would be inappropriate to touch include anywhere in the genital area and breasts. Touching in those areas is supposed to be reserved for marriage, which is clear from Song of Solomon and Ezekiel 23:1-3. Basically, don't touch any body part that you don't have yourself. *Being touched by a doctor for medical purposes does not qualify as inappropriate touch*

on, being naked with your significant other even if there's no touching involved, and talking "dirty" or having phone sex.[56]

You may think that the list is a bit extreme, but according to the Bible, those fall into the categories of sexually immoral things that are not permissible outside of marriage.[57] As mentioned in Chapter 9, our bodies are temples of the Holy Spirit;[58] they belong to God, and we need to live in a way that respects the sacredness of that. Exposing your body to people and giving it away freely is not something that should be done nonchalantly. Being sexually intimate with someone is supposed to be a special moment between you and your spouse. Because of that, the boundaries that I mentioned are important and shouldn't be taken lightly. I say all of that because none of those activities outside of marriage will strengthen your relationship with God or glorify Him. From what I have seen in my own experiences and the experiences of others, those behaviors only distance you from God.

With that in mind, ultimately, the boundaries that you set in your relationship are between you, your significant other, and God. It isn't something that someone can decide for you. Aside from the lines that are definitely not appropriate to cross, there are some things that people feel varying levels of conviction about. For instance, some couples feel convicted about kissing in general; others feel convicted about kissing for too long, etc. Since it is unclear, we must be purposeful about asking God for

---

[56] Even though you aren't engaging in any physical sexual activity, talking about sex and what you want to do descriptively with your significant other is not okay. Yes, you aren't technically acting out on your desires, but your heart is not in the right place and things of that nature should only be shared between spouses. Matthew 5:28 demonstrates that entertaining inappropriate sexual thoughts is sinful even if you don't act on them.

[57] Adultery, pornography, and masturbation are not permissible in marriage either.

[58] 1 Corinthians 6:18–20.

wisdom and for softened hearts to recognize and follow our convictions.

For those of you that are struggling to determine if certain things that weren't listed earlier are okay, ask yourself the following questions:

- If a trusted mentor/accountability partner asked you what your physical boundaries were, would you feel comfortable telling them, or does the thought of telling someone else spark shame or conviction?
- Let's say you ended up breaking up with your significant other, and you marry someone else. Would you be able to be completely honest about telling your spouse about how far you had gone physically in other relationships or would you have a difficult time telling the truth?
- Do you feel uncomfortable when crossing certain boundaries, or do you find yourself repeatedly questioning whether a certain line is okay to cross?

Those are just a few questions to get you thinking. The point of them is to help you examine the motives behind your actions and the condition of your heart in relation to your obedience or disobedience to the convictions that God has placed on your heart. If you do something that you know is wrong or do something you aren't sure is okay, you need to stop, step back, and reevaluate. According to Romans 14:23b, if you don't follow your convictions (what you feel the Holy Spirit is telling you is right or wrong), you're sinning. In areas that you still feel unsure, I recommend that you take time to pray about it and have a serious conversation with your significant other.[59]

Now, what do you do when you and your significant other aren't on the same page about what's appropriate and what isn't? As I mentioned, people do have different personal convictions on certain boundaries, and that is okay. As long as the convictions the person says they are feeling don't go against any of the clear boundaries from earlier, neither of you would be in the wrong by having different convictions; it just means that God is calling you to different things. The important thing to remember if you have differing views is that you should not cause your significant other to feel pressured to lower their boundary standards to where you are at or vice versa.

In situations where couples feel like they are on different pages as far as what should be allowed, the right thing to do is to follow whatever the person with the stricter boundaries feels is okay. As believers, we are supposed to encourage each other to follow our convictions, not cause each other to stumble.[60] In situations where you or your significant other have the desire to please God in your relationship but find yourselves not feeling or at least not recognizing conviction about doing something

---

[59] Conversations about boundaries should happen in the right setting. You are more likely to justify certain boundaries if you talk about them after you and your significant other were just kissing, cuddling late at night, etc. These things should be talked about when you are wide awake and are not caught up in the emotions of being physical with each other. Be wise about the setting of the conversation. A good way to start it off would be by praying to God for wisdom and guidance as you navigate your relationship.

[60] Romans 14:13; Hebrews 10:24; If your significant other is pressuring you to go further than you feel comfortable with, I would encourage you to pray about whether you should be in a relationship with them in the first place. Pressuring, coercing, guilting, or shaming someone into doing more sexually is not love- it is wrong and selfish, and that is not something that should be tolerated.

that clearly violates what is appropriate, pray about why your hearts aren't lining up with God's. Have you fallen into the trap of justification or have you simply silenced your convictions and allowed your fleshly desires to overrule them? If you have, you can make the decision to change things today. All it takes is to bring your sin before God, repent, and accept the forgiveness that he freely offers. Once you are forgiven, you are called to walk in that freedom; any feelings of condemnation are not from God.[61]

Once you decide what boundaries you need to set in order to please God, where do you go from there? The following few tips can help:

- **Don't put yourselves in compromising situations:** If you know that a certain place or situation increases your feelings of temptation, you need to avoid them whenever possible. If being home alone is too much or hanging out past a certain time makes you more likely to do something you shouldn't do, you need to be mindful of that and not purposefully allow yourselves to be in those situations if you can help it. Everyone has different things that increase their sexual desires, so it is vital that you address them when you realize what they are.
- **Accountability partners:** As uncomfortable as it may seem, having a mentor or trusted friend who is a strong Christian speak into your life and hold you accountable can really help. This is not an easy battle, and we can't fight it alone. Having a person outside of your relationship to go to can help keep you in check by them providing an honest, unbiased view of your

[61] Romans 8:1–2; John 8:36.

actions/behaviors in your relationship. It's also helpful to have someone to encourage you and pray with you when you are struggling. Admitting to someone that you are having a difficult time with boundaries, are facing temptation, or have acted on your desires can be intimidating, but there is freedom in bringing the truth out into the light. Accountability partners are not supposed to make you feel ashamed for what you've done. They are supposed to help pick you up when you are down and remind you of the grace that God offers when you repent.[62]

- **Be honest and address struggles with keeping boundaries:** You can't fight temptation if you don't acknowledge that it's there. If you want to stay on top of your boundaries, you will need to have some tough, open, and possibly uncomfortable conversations with your significant other about where you are at in terms of your convictions. If doing something that you both said was okay is starting to become more of a turn on, you need to tell them that. Your significant other can't help you if they don't know that it is an issue. When having these conversations, it shouldn't be a conversation centered on, "these are the things that I want to do with you." It should be, "this is an area that we need to reevaluate or a boundary that we need to change because it is causing me to want to do more than we should." Having discussions about sex will make you feel closer and more intimate with your significant other which can spark desire for people, so it is important to keep the depth of the talk at an appropriate level.

---

62 1Thessalonians 5:11.

- **Stay on top of it:** Don't let your fight for purity fall to the wayside as you become more comfortable with each other. Have conversations periodically to check in and see where you are both at. Feelings and desires grow stronger as the relationship progresses, and you feel closer, so this isn't a one-time talk.
- **Remember that wanting to have sex is not bad or something to be ashamed of**. Wanting to have a sexual relationship with your significant other or desiring sex is not wrong; it's natural. However, we are not supposed to act on our desires (until marriage) or allow them to consume our thoughts. Understanding the distinction helps us view sex in a positive light while reminding us that it is meant to be allowed and embraced in marriage and marriage alone.
- **Spend time building your relationship with God daily**. As I said before, the only way that we can truly follow God's plan for purity in our hearts, minds, and bodies is by pursuing Him above all else and spending time with Him. Take time each day to talk to Him and to get to know Him more. Reading your Bible, doing a short devotional, praying, and listening to worship songs are just a few ways to do that. In order to fully follow God, we have to be able to recognize His voice, which takes time and practice. Be honest with Him about your struggles and ask Him to show you how He wants you to live. I promise that if you seek Him with all of your heart, you will find Him.[63]

I know that this chapter was a lot to take in, and you may not agree with everything that I said. As I've said before, these are

[63] Deuteronomy 4:29; Jeremiah 29:13.

conclusions that I have reached after lots of prayer and careful consideration of Scriptures. You may feel differently about it, and that's okay. Some things might not have sat right with you, and for those things, I encourage you to search the Bible for yourself and ask God for discernment as you seek His guidance. If anything, I hope that this chapter at the very least sparks your desire to consider making the decision to go against the flow by daring to date differently.

Reflection and Application

1. What do you think are appropriate boundaries?
2. Are there any areas of your physical boundaries that you need to reevaluate and change so that you are better following your convictions?
3. Do you have an accountability partner to help you as you walk through this journey? If not, pray about asking someone to be your accountability partner this week. If you are a couple reading this book, consider asking a married Christian couple to mentor you together.
4. If you are in a relationship, have a conversation with your significant other about your thoughts on this chapter and how you feel, applying it in the context of being a couple and as individuals.
5. Pray this week specifically that God will soften your heart to hear His instruction and that your eyes will be open to anything that you need to change. Ask Him to give you the strength to flee from temptation, to show you how to glorify Him, and to remove anything that is hindering you from living how He is calling you to live.

How to Date Well

Dating can be an exciting time in your life that God can use to ultimately lead you to find the person that you are going to marry one day. When you first start dating, your relationship might seem to be fueled by the butterfly feelings that you get when you see your significant other. Once the initial excitement and newness of the relationship wears off, some people tend to say that the "honeymoon phase" of the relationship has ended. While I do think that's true to an extent, from my own experience, I believe that you can still have a fulfilling and exciting relationship as time goes on. The key to maintaining a strong relationship is similar to the key to having a strong relationship with Christ: being purposeful.

Being purposeful means not simply going through the motions, but actively participating in your relationship, even when you don't feel like it. It means making an effort to spend quality time with each other and checking in with each other to see how you both are doing. Spending time together and communicating with each other should be more than a check on your list of things to do; it should be something that you both make a priority and work towards.[64] Being purposeful requires patience, determination, selflessness, and creativity.

[64] I have included a list of date ideas at the end of this chapter to give you some ideas.

Sometimes, your circumstances can make being purposeful in your relationship difficult. Christian and I learned this when I went away to college, and he went to a local college. Having a long-distance relationship (even though we were only 2 ½ hours away) was a challenge and required us to do a lot of adjusting. Given the time zone differences and our busy schedules, we had to be extremely purposeful about setting time aside to call or Facetime each other or to choose weekends that we could visit each other. One of the biggest things I learned through that season of long-distance was to always make the most out of the time that we had together. Small talk quickly shifted into deep conversations about our faith, fears, struggles, and hopes for the future.

Early on in our time of dating long-distance, we agreed that another thing that we needed to be purposeful about is putting and keeping Christ at the center of our relationship. First, we established the importance of each of us having a daily personal relationship with Jesus on our own. Then, we were able to continue to grow closer to God together. We found that praying together and separately for each other, and our relationship helped us grow immensely. When we were at a place in our relationship where we didn't know when we would be able to get married (or if that was even God's plan for us), we prayed. When we would have disagreements with each other and struggled to reach a compromise, we prayed. When we faced days where dating long-distance was really difficult, and days when sadness felt overwhelming, we prayed. When we felt closer to each other and to God, we prayed. When God gave us favor in school and work, we prayed. Through the good and the bad, we would pour our hearts out to God, thanking Him for all He has done and seeking His guidance in all areas of our lives. I want to encourage you to do the same.

Similarly, to keep our relationship centered on Christ, Christian and I chose to find devotional/study books for Christian couples. Normally, we would bring the book with us to the beach, a nature trail, or a local park and read a chapter at a time on our dates. Reading those books helped us learn a lot about each other and gave us advice and information that strengthened our relationship. It allowed us to reflect and take time to think about deeper questions instead of sticking with small talk. By the end of each book, I found that we had both taken what we read and had begun applying it to our daily lives, which improved our relationship as a couple and our relationships with others.[65]

There are also a few other things that I have learned that are key to dating well. One of the biggest things that I learned was avoiding co-dependence. Co-dependence is essentially when you and your significant other get so caught up in your relationship that you begin to lose sight of who you are as individuals. Co-dependence can also lead some couples to neglect their family and their friends, which is not healthy. I strongly believe that you can find a healthy balance between the time spent in your dating relationship and the other areas of your life. At times, that requires compromises on both ends. Maybe instead of going out on a date one night, you both decide to spend the evening with one of your families or you go on a group outing with some of your friends. Community is an important part of our lives, and we should be careful not to push everyone else away even though we may want to spend all of our free time with our significant other.

I had some friends in high school that became co-dependent when they were dating someone. They pushed all

---

[65] I have provided a list of books that I recommend you read as a couple or even individually at the end of this book.

of their friends and family away and always said that they were too busy to hang out with other people. Eventually, they broke up and saw that they didn't have anyone to turn to because they had neglected them during their entire relationship. My advice—your friends and especially your family are more than likely going to be some of the main "constants" in your life. Don't push them to the wayside. Continue to cultivate your friendships and relationships so, that even if you and your significant other break up or if you simply need relationship advice, you still have people available to support you and encourage you.

Staying well-rounded is a great way to ensure that you have balance in your relationship. If you haven't already, I would encourage you to figure out what your interests are and to participate in activities that fit those interests. Whether that means participating in extracurricular activities like sports or clubs, volunteering, or having a job, it is good to be involved in something that you enjoy and that you chose because you wanted to do it, not only because your significant other is involved in it. Doing so can help both of you continue to solidify your identities as individuals, which also prevents co-dependence. This doesn't mean that you can't do things together that you both enjoy. I just think that is it healthy to help you make sure that you do not lose who you are in your relationship.

Another good way to maintain your individual identity is by making it a priority to have time for yourself. Personally, I like to have time to journal, listen to music, read, or play the piano. For Christian, that means taking time to go on a bike ride, workout, roller skate, or work on a project at home or in his dad's workshop. Taking time for yourself looks different for each person, and I want you to really think about what that looks like for you.

Lastly, if you feel that God is/may be calling you in separate directions, I want you to know that I realize how difficult that can be. I also want to encourage you to not make any choices that would cause you to stray away from that path God is leading you to, even if that means going away from your significant other. Christian and I lived that out and dated long distance for two years. It wasn't easy, but it strengthened our relationship and helped us grow and develop better communication skills. My prayer is that, if you are facing a similar situation, God will give you wisdom and that He will use that season of your life to help you mature and learn to lean on Him more. I also pray that you and your significant other are purposeful about going to God for guidance when making those big decisions.

Date Ideas

- Going on a nature trail
- Watching the sunrise/sunset
- Go on a picnic
- Go on a bike ride
- Antique or thrift store shopping
- Explore the Mainstreet of your town
- Geocaching
- Dinner and a movie
- Game night
- Photoshoot
- Cooking together
- Ice or roller skating
- Double dates/group dates
- Mini golf
- Laser tag
- Escape room
- Find a café/coffee shop

- Shopping
- Bowling
- Volunteer
- Dance lessons
- Go to the beach
- Study together
- Volunteering or serving in church

Reflection and Application

1. What are some ways that you like to take time for yourself?
2. What are your hopes/dreams for the future?
3. a) Are you being purposeful in your relationship and friendships?
   b) If not, what are some ways that you can start being more purposeful?
4. Do you have any other date ideas or were there any ideas that were mentioned above that stood out to you?
5. Choose a new hobby that you would like to try or an old hobby that you've missed doing and take some time for yourself this week.
6. Reach out to a friend that you haven't seen lately and spend some quality time with them.

Building the Kingdom

> Therefore, go and make disciples of all the nations, baptizing them in the name of the Father and the Son and the Holy Spirit.
>
> Matthew 28:19 (NLT)

I believe that this message is very straightforward and applicable not only to dating relationships but in relation to the call that we have on our lives as Christians. I'll start off by asking you to think: What should be the main goal of dating? While there are a few purposes of dating that we have talked about throughout the book, ultimately, your goal should be to grow closer to Christ as you grow closer to each other.

How do you do that? One of the best ways is to work to serve the Lord side-by-side. That means relentlessly pursuing Christ over your own interests; loving God with all your hearts, souls, and minds; loving your neighbors as yourselves; working willingly at whatever you do as if you were doing it for the Lord; and looking to the interests of others. [66] Hold each other accountable in truth and love, and push each other to go past your comfort zones, even when it's uncomfortable or inconvenient.

---

[66] Mark 12:30-31; Colossians 3:23; Philippians 2:4.

Living for Jesus may look different depending on the person. I believe that each person has a unique call on their life, a mission that they were specifically created to accomplish. There is no role too small, every person plays an important part in building.[67] One of my mentors in college said it best, "Different bait catches different fish." We each have unique personality traits that God can use to reach people that others might not have been able to.

Obediently serving the Lord doesn't necessarily mean that God will ask you to move to a foreign country to be a missionary.[68] God can use you right where you are, no matter what type of influence you think you have or what your perceived qualifications may be. In fact, I think God is less concerned about where you are and what career you will pursue and is more concerned about if your heart is in the right place and you are seeking Him above all else with the desire to serve Him in whatever way He asks you to. So before calling it quits when it comes to living for Christ because it seems intimidating, know that God will be with you every step of the way.

Once you make the decision to live for Jesus wholeheartedly as an individual and in your relationship, it is important to ask yourself the following questions:

- What do I think God is calling me to do?
- What are my spiritual gifts?[69]
- Where do I feel God is calling me to serve right now? (missions, homeless ministry, children's church, local soup kitchen, campus ministry, etc.)
- How can I actively walk in obedience as I pursue what God is asking me to do?

---

67 1 Corinthians 12:12–26.

68 Although that is a call that some people have on their lives, it is not for everyone.

69 Romans 12:6–8;1 Corinthians 12:6–10.

Discussing those questions with a trusted mentor and your significant other can be very beneficial once you've had time to reflect and ask God about it on your own. Thinking and praying about if God is leading you both in the same direction can help strengthen your relationship and give you a clearer idea of where God is taking you individually and as a couple.

As daunting as it may sound, I also challenge you to go into those discussions with the mindset of choosing God over your significant other, if that's what following your calling requires. Christian and I had some tough discussions about that early on in our relationship, and even more in-depth when our relationship became long-distance once I moved away for college, unsure whether God was taking us in the same direction. While it was difficult, we submitted our relationship to God and prayed that His will would be done over our own and that He would guide us to whatever would bring Him the most glory, even if that meant going our separate ways and breaking up.

At the time, we were still only dating, and we didn't know if our relationship would last. Although we both wanted it to and prayed for it to work out, there were still a lot of unknowns about the future. We didn't find peace and answers confirming that God was leading us to get married for a while, which left us in a season of walking by faith in full submission in the meantime. I don't know if you've been in a similar situation, if you are currently, or if you will be in the future, but I do know this: God is faithful and will give you wisdom in His perfect timing regarding your relationship if you ask for it.[70] The one thing you need to make sure you are prepared to follow through with is doing whatever He tells you to do. We can find hope in this as well—if you are meant to be with the person you are in a relationship with, God will work it out. As cliché as that sounds,

[70] James 1:5.

it's the truth, and I encourage you to remember that when you aren't sure what direction your relationship is heading.

Now that we've addressed surrendering to how God wants to use us, let's focus on how you can build God's Kingdom through your relationship. The great thing about being in a relationship centered on Christ is that you can encourage each other to serve in the capacity that God is calling you to. I think that it may even be one of the most fulfilling parts of a godly relationship. By sharing the heart to walk in obedience to God, you can serve alongside each other and grow tremendously in your faith.

For example, you can volunteer together, join or even lead a Bible study, meet up with other couples that are Christians to encourage each other and learn from each other and spend time reflecting on what God has been showing you lately in your devotional time with Him. As I talked about in earlier chapters, living for Jesus means surrendering every part of your life to Him and inviting Him to move freely in and through you, however He sees fit.

Reflection and Application

1. Is there a way that you can step into the calling that God has placed in your life this week?
2. a) What are some of the spiritual gifts that God has given you? See Romans 12:6–8 and 1 Corinthians 12:6–10 for examples.

   b) How can you use those gifts to serve others?
3. Plan an activity in which you (and your significant other if you have one) can help build the Kingdom.
4. Spend time this week asking God to give you wisdom about the direction that He is taking you in and discuss it with your significant other or a trusted mentor or friend.

Love is…

> Love is patient, love is kind. It does not envy, it does not boast, it is not proud. It does not dishonor others, it is not self-seeking, it is not easily angered, it keeps no record of wrongs. Love does not delight in evil but rejoices with the truth. It always protects, always trusts, always hopes, always perseveres. Love never fails.
>
> —1 Corinthians 13:4-8a

Love. It is a word that carries so much meaning, yet it can be used carelessly. In today's culture, love is everywhere—our love for food, the latest movie, the new album from our favorite music artist, etc. That "love" that we have for things of this world is much different than the love that we have for the people in our lives: our friends, family, and significant others. When love is overused, it can diminish some of its meaning, which is why it's important to use it wisely and to truly understand its definition.

Knowing that, what exactly is the meaning of love? Love is more than a feeling; it is a choice that you must make each day, regardless of the circumstances. The Bible provides us with several examples of what love is and what it looks like when lived out. The greatest example of love by far was Jesus dying on the cross for us—a sinless man that gave his life to save the world while we were still sinners. Jesus also demonstrates his love for people in the way that he cared for and served people of all backgrounds. Seeing how Jesus loved us is inspiring. When trying to live that out in our own lives though, we can hit a roadblock, unsure of what loving others should look like in today's society. The good news is that 1 Corinthians 13:4–8 gives us some guidelines. Here is a breakdown of the verse to make it more applicable to your life:

Love is:

- **Patient**: having the capacity to accept or tolerate delay, trouble, or suffering without getting angry or upset.[71] Be patient with your significant other when they are struggling with something or are going through a difficult time. A relationship is not always going to seem like it's 50/50. Sometimes, it will seem like it's 75/25 when your significant other has to lean on you because they can't do it on their own. When it comes to dealing with difficult and stressful situations or disagreements, remember that getting angry may make the situation worse, so do your best to listen to them, validate their feelings, and focus on the problem at hand rather than getting upset with each other. Extend grace to them the way that God does for you.
- **Kind**: the quality of being friendly, generous, and considerate. Even when you don't feel like it, you are called to be kind. Try to find little ways to be kind to others: open doors for people, help an elderly

[71] *Oxford English Dictionary,* 2nd ed. (Oxford: Oxford University Press, 2004), s.v. "Patience."

person carry their groceries to their car, compliment/ encourage someone, or simply check in to see how someone is doing. Being kind does not always require a ton of effort, but it can have a lasting, positive impact that could change someone's life.

- **Trusting:** In a loving relationship, you should be able to trust your significant other, and they should be able to trust you. The key to building trust is to be open and vulnerable with each other, not deliberately hiding parts of yourself. Trust takes time to form as your relationship progresses, but it is important to remember that it can be broken quickly. Do your best to make others feel comfortable with trusting you by keeping things that they share with you to yourself and by being there for them when they are seeking biblical advice.
- **Hopeful:** One of the best parts of loving someone is that you get to dream and hope together. Remind each other of the promises that God has spoken over your lives and encourage each other in the midst of adversity and trials. If your significant other is struggling, try to help them find hope in their situation.

Love also:

- **Keeps No Record of Wrongs:** In the same way that God forgives us of our sins and wipes our slates clean, we need to forgive others.[72] This also means that we are not supposed to hold grudges or keep bringing up

[72] Colossians 3:13.

our significant other's wrongdoings over and over after we forgive them.

- **Rejoices with the Truth:** Celebrate each other's growth in your faith and personal lives. Share the truth of what God has done in your life with those around you, and do not be shy about being who God created you to be.
- **Protects:** We are called to protect each other's hearts and to watch out for each other's spiritual wellbeing. Be mindful of treating your significant other the way that you would want to be treated. Be careful not to be careless with their heart and feelings. Instead, do your best to be considerate and to protect them from emotional harm. As believers and in relationships, we are supposed to have each other's backs.
- **Perseveres:** Don't automatically give up when things get difficult. You will have hard times in your relationship, times when you argue and don't get along, times when you aren't sure how things are going to work out. Having disagreements is normal and even healthy in a relationship because it means that you are communicating. The important thing is how you argue. When you go through hard times in life and in your relationship, the important thing is to view it as you and your significant other versus the problem not the two of you against each other. When you face a problem, keep pressing on by leaning on each other and God.
- **Never Fails:** we are called to imitate the love that God has for us, which is unconditional and never fails. God's love for us is not dependent on who we are or what we do. His love is freely and generously given to all who seek Him. As we enter friendships and relationships,

we are to remember His sacrificial love and to strive to exhibit that in our own lives.

Love is not:

- **Envious:** feeling or showing the desire to have a quality, possession, or other desirable attribute belonging to someone else.[73] It can be easy to fall into the comparison trap, to feel unworthy or lesser when comparing yourself to the people around you. However, to exhibit real love, we should stop trying to compete with other people and start embracing our own strengths and who God created us to be. By focusing on building each other up instead of tearing ourselves or others down, we can love without letting envy get in the way.
- **Boastful or Prideful:** having an extremely high view of oneself, sometimes in a bragging manner. A loving person does their best to avoid being boastful/prideful and instead aims to be humble. One of the best ways I've heard humility described is that it is not thinking less of yourself. Humility is thinking of yourself less.
- **Easily Angered:** Being angry can lead to sin if not handled appropriately.[74] Feeling angry is not the problem; it's a normal emotion. However, the problem with being angry lies in how we handle and act on that emotion. Rather than allowing our anger to lead us

---

[73] *Oxford English Dictionary,* 2nd ed. (Oxford: Oxford University Press, 2004), s.v. "Envious."

[74] Ephesians 4:26.

to lash out and treat people poorly, we should exhibit self-control.

- **Self-seeking:** To avoid being self-seeking or selfish, you should look to others' interests over your own.[75] In a relationship, that means that there will be times that you have to make compromises and sacrifices for your significant other. That may be as simple as letting them choose what to do on a date night or more difficult like being the bigger person by conceding in an argument for the sake of your relationship. Having a heart to serve instead of being served is imperative to loving well.

Love does not:

- **Dishonor Others:** One of the most important things in a relationship is to do your best to honor your significant other in the way that you treat them. A part of that is by honoring them through striving for purity both physically and spiritually. Honoring each other means pushing each other to be who God has created you to be, treating each other with respect, and loving them the way that Christ does.
- **Delight in Evil:** To put this one simply, Romans 12:21 (NLT) says, *"don't let evil conquer you, but conquer evil by doing good."* Living in love means killing our enemies with kindness and doing good no matter how difficult that may be.

As you can see, love is so much more than a fleeting emotion. Love is one of the most important elements of being a Christian.

---

[75] Philippians 2:4.

As you interact with your family, friends, significant others, and yes, even strangers, do your best to love. My prayer for you is that you love fiercely and freely with reckless abandon, holding nothing back. I pray that the love that you have for others shines and that, in turn, people see Jesus when they look at you. Loving people the way Christ did is not easy by any means, but that's a part of daring to date differently and not conforming to the world. I hope you make the decision to love radically today and that your love for others grows as your love for God deepens.

<u>Reflection and Application</u>

1. How can you improve living out your love for God and the people in your life?
2. a) Do you fit the characteristics that describe love?
   b) Are there any areas of your life that don't line up with what living in love should look like?
3. Does your relationship exhibit the love that Christ has for us?
4. Pick one characteristic that you would like to improve on and find a way to practice living it out each day for the entire week. At the end of the week, reflect on how you did and if you feel a change in your heart.

Conclusion

As this book comes to a close, I hope that you feel better equipped to dare to date differently by relentlessly pursuing Christ no matter the cost. Remember to go to God about all things, including your dating life. Nothing is insignificant to Him, and He pays attention to every single detail of your life. Luke 12:7 even says that God knows the number of hairs on your head.

Daring to date differently is one of the most challenging, yet best decisions that you can ever make. There may be times when you stumble, but God will be there to pick you back up and put you back on track. When it comes down to it, He simply wants you to have a heart that yearns to live for Him and for you to die to yourself and your flesh as you pursue the desires of the Holy Spirit.

With that, I want to leave you with my prayer for you, the same prayer that Paul had for the body of believers that he wrote to who lived in Colossae, which can be found in Colossians 1:9b–12:

> *We continually ask God to fill you with the knowledge of His will through all the wisdom and understanding that the Spirit gives, so that you may live a life worthy of the Lord and please Him in every way: bearing fruit in every*

> *good work, growing in the knowledge of God, being strengthened with all power according to His glorious might so that you may have great endurance and patience, and giving joyful thanks to the Father, who has qualified you to share in the inheritance of His holy people in the kingdom of light.*

As you enter this season of dating and preparing for marriage, I encourage you to pursue Christ with all that you are, holding nothing back. Know that I am continuously praying for you and praying that God equips you and encourages you as you step out in faith boldly to not conform to the patterns of this world by allowing the Holy Spirit to guide you. I am cheering you on in spirit as you walk this difficult journey, and I am so proud of you and your heart to serve God and live a life of surrender.

Love,
Haleigh

Recommended Books

- *Swipe Right: The Life and Death Power of Romance* by Levi Lusko
- *Single, Dating, Engaged, Married: Navigating Life and Love in the Modern Age* by Ben Stuart
- *Your Story, Our Story: Intentionally Dating on Purpose* by Tyler Moore
- *Whatever is... A Couple's Devotional for Christian Dating in a Secular World* by Ryan C. Vet
- *The Five Love Languages* by Gary Chapman

www.ingramcontent.com/pod-product-compliance
Ingram Content Group UK Ltd.
Pitfield, Milton Keynes, MK11 3LW, UK
UKHW040019200726
13854UKWH00001B/271

9 781664 209473